Learn About Rural Life

Life in a Farming Community

Lizann Flatt

Crabtree Publishing Company
www.crabtreebooks.com

Author: Lizann Flatt
Editor-in-Chief: Lionel Bender
Editors: Simon Adams and Molly Aloian
Proofreader: Crystal Sikkens
Editorial director: Kathy Middleton
Photo research: Lizann Flatt and Ben White
Designer: Ben White
Production coordinator: Katherine Berti
Production: Kim Richardson
Prepress technician: Margaret Amy Salter
Consultant: Heather L. Montgomery, DragonFly
    Environmental Education Programs

Front cover (main image): A dairy farm in
    Wisconsin, U.S.A.
Back cover: A young girl with her horse
Title page: Farm buildings on a farm in
    Green County, Wisconsin, U.S.A.

This book was produced for Crabtree Publishing
Company by Bender Richardson White.

Photographs and reproductions
Corbis Images: Alvis Upitis: p. 23
Marc Crabtree: front cover (inset)
Getty Images: p. 19, 21, 24; National Geographic: p. 25
greencountyspotlight.com: Polly L. Brockert: p. 12, 15,
    16, 17, 27; Richard M. Grahn: p. 13, 18, 20, 22, 26
Istockphoto: page corner graphic, p. 1, 4, 5, 6, 7, 8, 9, 11,
    14, 28, 29
Shutterstock: front cover (main image), back cover
Topfoto: The Granger Collection: p. 10

Acknowledgments
Special thanks to:
Richard M. Grahn of Green County Spotlight LLC for
supplying many of the photographs of Monticello used
in this book.
Sally Braem, owner of Extended Stay Rooming House in
Monticello, for checking and advising on the local
information.
Cover models Allan Ivey, Alissa Lefebvre, Aimee
Lefebvre, Kyle Foxton, and Zach Sikkens.

Library and Archives Canada Cataloguing in Publication

Flatt, Lizann
    Life in a farming community / Lizann Flatt.

(Learn about rural life)
Includes index.
ISBN 978-0-7787-5071-0 (bound).--ISBN 978-0-7787-5084-0 (pbk.)

    1. Farm life--Juvenile literature. 2. Dairying--Juvenile
literature. 3. Cheesemakers--Juvenile literature. 4. Monticello
(Wis.)--Juvenile literature. I. Title. II. Series: Learn about
rural life

S519.F53 2009   j630   C2009-903742-4

Library of Congress Cataloging-in-Publication Data

Flatt, Lizann.
    Life in a farming community / Lizann Flatt.
        p. cm. -- (Learn about rural life)
    Includes index.
    ISBN 978-0-7787-5084-0 (pbk. : alk. paper)
    -- ISBN 978-0-7787-5071-0 (reinforced library binding : alk. paper)
    1. Farm life--Wisconsin--Monticello--Juvenile literature. 2.
Dairying--Wisconsin--Monticello--Juvenile literature. 3.
Cheesemakers--Wisconsin--Monticello--Social conditions--
Juvenile literature. I. Title. II. Series.

    S521.5.W6F55 2009
    630.9775'86--dc22

                                    2009023640

Crabtree Publishing Company

www.crabtreebooks.com   1-800-387-7650
Copyright © **2010 CRABTREE PUBLISHING COMPANY.** All rights reserved. No part of this publication may be
reproduced, stored in a retrieval system or be transmitted in any form or by any means, electronic, mechanical,
photocopying, recording, or otherwise, without the prior written permission of Crabtree Publishing Company. In
Canada: We acknowledge the financial support of the Government of Canada through the Book Publishing Industry
Development Program (BPIDP) for our publishing activities.

**Published
in Canada**
Crabtree Publishing
616 Welland Ave.
St. Catharines, Ontario
L2M 5V6

**Published in
the United States**
Crabtree Publishing
PMB16A
350 Fifth Ave., Suite 3308
New York, NY 10118

**Published in the
United Kingdom**
Crabtree Publishing
White Cross Mills
High Town, Lancaster
LA1 4XS

**Published
in Australia**
Crabtree Publishing
386 Mt. Alexander Rd.
Ascot Vale (Melbourne)
VIC 3032

Contents

A Rural Community

Many people live and work in cities and big towns. They are surrounded by tall buildings, busy streets, a lot of stores, and many neighbors. These places are called **urban areas**. Other people live in villages and small towns. These places have fewer people and stores. The buildings are lower, and the streets are quieter. They are surrounded by countryside. These are **rural areas**.

▼ A large city such as Boston, Massachusetts, is an urban area. Nearly 600,000 people live here.

Farm buildings surrounded by fields close to a village. In the countryside, it is much quieter and less busy than in a city.

Farms are found in rural areas on large fields in the countryside. They are usually far from urban areas. Most farmers live in or near villages. The people in and around a village live, work, and play together. They form a **community**. In a rural area, there is one community. In a city, there may be many separate communities. This book looks at life in a rural area that relies mostly on farming.

What is Farming?

Farming is **raising** or growing something so that it can be sold to others. There are two main types of farming—**livestock** and **crop**. Livestock farms raise animals such as cows, pigs, chickens, **alpacas**, and horses. Crop farms grow plants producing fruits, vegetables, and grains. Some farms raise livestock and grow crops.

▼ This farmer looks at his field of wheat. Crops such as wheat, barley, oats, and corn produce grains that we eat as breakfast cereals or make into flour for bread, cakes, and pasta.

Plants need sunlight and water to grow. Livestock needs to be fed. Farmers always have to look after their land and animals. In dry times, the land may need to be **irrigated**, or watered. Fields need to be **plowed** to **sow** seeds and so that the soil will not wash away in heavy rains. **Pests** that eat plants may need to be killed. Animals must be taken out to fields to eat or brought indoors and fed.

What Comes from a Farm?

The crops and livestock that a farmer sells are known as **farm products**. Fruits, vegetables, meats, and grains are sold as food. Wool from sheep or alpacas is **spun** into yarn to make sweaters and carpets. Cotton and flax plants make **fibers** from which we make cotton and linen cloth. Milk from cows is sold as a drink and to make **dairy foods**.

▼ All kinds of fruits and vegetables are sold at food markets.

Some farms are now growing plants from which **fuels** are made. Others are using animal and plant wastes from their farms to make electricity. No matter where people live, they need food, fresh water, materials to build their homes, and energy to light and heat their homes. Farmers provide these things to people in urban areas who cannot easily grow or make these products themselves.

Farming in North America began with the native peoples who grew foods such as corn or squash. As **settlers** arrived, many of them grew crops and raised livestock to feed their families. During the next few hundred years, settlers set up farms everywhere. Machines such as the combine were invented to make farm work easier and faster. With these new machines, fewer people were needed to do the work.

▼ Starting around 1850, thousands of people moved west and set up farms and homes on the plains and prairies. At first, they could make only enough food to feed themselves.

A combine harvests wheat on the Great Plains. It cuts the wheat and collects the grains in a pan. Then the wheat stems, called straw, are dropped back out onto the field. Straw is used as bedding for farm animals.

The Canadian Prairies and the Great Plains region of the United States are where most cereal crops are grown. Cattle **ranches** and large farms can be found in these places, too. A lot of fruits and vegetables grow in California. Florida produces **citrus** fruits. Tobacco, peanuts, soybeans, and cotton grow in the South. The Midwest is known for corn and other grains. Dairy farming and livestock farms are important in many regions of the East.

Monticello is a village in Green County located in southern Wisconsin in the United States. About 1,200 people live in the village. Monticello is surrounded by farmland. Today, there are many different kinds of farms here, such as dairy, mountain elk, horse, and alpaca farms. Several cheese factories are also important to the village.

▼ This sign sits alongside the road into the village. Monticello is very rural. The nearest city, Madison, is around 30 miles (49 km) away.

▲ The village of Monticello as seen from the air.

Farmers first settled this area in the mid-1800s. Many set up dairy farms. **Factories** were soon built and the milk was used to make cheese. The area became known for its **Limburger** and **Swiss cheeses**. A railroad once ran through the area. A train, nicknamed the *Limburger Special*, stopped to pick up the cheeses so they could be sold all over the country.

Life in Monticello

Many people who live in Monticello work on local farms or make farm products. Others work in local businesses, small stores, offices, or at the school. Throughout the year, children play basketball, volleyball, and football. In the summer, they swim in the pool and ride their bikes. The community library has books, DVDs, CDs, computers, and information for everyone.

▼ Children board one of the school buses. The elementary, middle, and high school are in one building in the village. About 350 children go to the school.

Lake Montesian is near the center of the village. It is an important attraction. Families kayak, canoe, or fish here in their spare time. People stroll through the paths in Montesian Gardens to enjoy all kinds of beautiful flowers. There are many spots for biking and hiking nearby. The village has banks, restaurants, services, and stores, many of which are on Main Street.

Monticello celebrates the seasons. In spring, the Apple Blossom Festival celebrates the flowering of the village's crab apple trees and the start to the growing season. In summer, a county fair takes place in the nearby town of Monroe to celebrate the **harvest**. Monticello farmers compete with their best farm products. There is also a rodeo, tractor pulls, and horse racing.

▼ When crab apple trees flower in May, Monticello celebrates the beauty the trees bring to the village.

In the summer, people celebrate the Homecoming festival with a carnival, games, fireworks, and a street parade.

In winter, Lake Montesian freezes over. Then the village holds its annual ice-fishing tournament. Holes are chopped in the ice and people fish through them. The catch is celebrated with a fish fry. One year, when the lake was being cleaned and the fish were removed, the village held a chicken barbecue instead.

A Farming Family

Most farms around Monticello are owned and run by local families. Each family lives in a house on their land, near the farm's barns, silos, and sheds. Animals live in, or take shelter in, the barns. Silos are used to store plant food needed to feed the animals. Farm equipment is kept in the sheds to protect it from the weather. Farm families do not have to travel far to be at work.

▼ This view of Monticello farms from the sky shows the different farm buildings, the houses, and the tall silos.

Children often help out with the work on the farm. This boy gives a week-old calf some milk to drink.

Farmers get up early in the morning because their animals are awake early and need to be fed and watered. They spend most of the day on the farm. They also spend time handling the business of the farm. Farmers do this from home. They use newpapers, TV, radio, and the Internet to keep track of the weather and the prices of farm products.

On the Farm

There are many jobs on a farm. Every day, the animals must be given food and water. Their barns need to be cleaned. Farmers use machines called tractors to make the job of moving big bales of hay or loads of **manure** much easier. Tractors also pull equipment that plow the land, sow seeds, and harvest crops.

▼ This tractor is pulling a baler. A baler is a machine that gathers up and bundles, or bales, the hay that was earlier cut and piled in rows.

▲ Crops such as wheat and soybeans are ready to harvest when they are fully grown and dried by the summer sun.

The crops are harvested once they are fully grown and ready to be used. On Monticello farms, most things are harvested only once a year. When crops such as winter wheat, soybeans, corn, or oats have grown, they are cut down. The grains are collected and stored. Most sheep and alpacas have their wool sheared, or cut off, once a year. The wool is spun and then sold.

On a Dairy Farm

On a dairy farm, cows must be milked two or three times a day. Farmers use milking machines to make this job faster. With these machines, many cows can be milked at once. The machines draw the milk from the cows, through hoses, and into big tanks.

▼ It is milking time, so these boys are putting the milking machine's cups on the cows' udders.

The tanks store the milk and keep it fresh and cold. Almost every day, a special milk truck visits the farm. The stored milk is pumped into the truck's tank. The truck collects milk from a few farms and then takes it to a local cheese factory or milk plant.

▲ The milk truck's tank is like a big cooler. It is used to keep the milk cold on the trip from the farm to a factory.

At the Processing Plant

Some farm products are taken to food **processing plants** in neighboring towns. Some people from Monticello work at the plants. Local fruits are canned or made into jams or sauces. Vegetables may be cut up, packed, and frozen for sale. Part of the corn crop is used as food for cattle. The rest is processed to make a fuel for cars.

▼ Some meats are ground into tiny pieces that are then seasoned and stuffed into casing to make sausages.

At a processing plant in Monticello, milk from local farms is made into cheese. Elsewhere in Green County, milk is used to make yogurt, butter, and ice cream.

At a meat-packing plant, workers inspect meat to be sure it is safe to eat. Most meats are sent to stores for people to buy and cook at home. Milk is taken to a factory where it is treated to kill any bacteria. Then it is put into cartons, bottles, or bags for people to buy.

Changing Lifestyle

Many North American farming communities like Monticello are finding it hard to survive. Farms do not always make enough money from selling their products. Farmland is expensive to buy and to look after. Today, many people in the village work in **construction** and trucking. Some farmers raise money by holding tours for visitors to see what happens on a farm.

▼ Boating, canoeing, and kayaking on Lake Montesian are popular pastimes for both visitors and local residents.

Just outside Monticello, an old, unused railroad route has been turned into an attractive biking and walking trail.

Monticello now attracts visitors who spend money on hotels, meals, and local activities. Each May, a local farm breakfast attracts 5,000 people. Visitors can also tour the cheese factories and buy cheese from their onsite stores. The State of Wisconsin has built trails near Monticello that attract cyclists and hikers in the summer and snowmobile riders and cross-country skiers in the winter.

Farming Around the World

Countries all over the world depend on their farms to feed their own people. The farms also make products that they sell to other countries. Foods that we enjoy in North America, such as sugar, cocoa for making chocolate, bananas, rice, coffee, and tea, often come from farms in other parts of the world.

▼ In China and other parts of Asia, rice is harvested by hand from fields known as paddies.

Not all farmers have tractors. Farmers near Gondal, India, use a pair of oxen to plow a field.

China and India grow the most fruits, vegetables, and cereal grains in the world. The grains include wheat, rice, oats, and corn. They also produce a lot of meat from cows, chickens, and pigs. Other big producers of fruits, vegetables, and grains are the United States, Brazil, Russia, and Spain. Countries that produce a lot of meats and dairy foods are Brazil, Germany, France, and New Zealand.

Facts and Figures

The farming industry
About one-third of workers in the world work on farms or make farm products. Many of them work on small farms. Farms fill more than one-third of all the land on Earth. The rest is mountains, forests, cities, roads, and lakes.

Farm products
One cow can produce 46,000 glasses of milk in a year. The average cow produces 2,100 lbs (953 kg) of milk each month. A person eats about 240 eggs in a year. This is about the number of eggs a chicken will lay each year.

Cheese production
The United States is the world's largest producer of cheese. However, France sells more cheese around the world than any other country. The French cheese factories produce more than 350 different types of cheese.

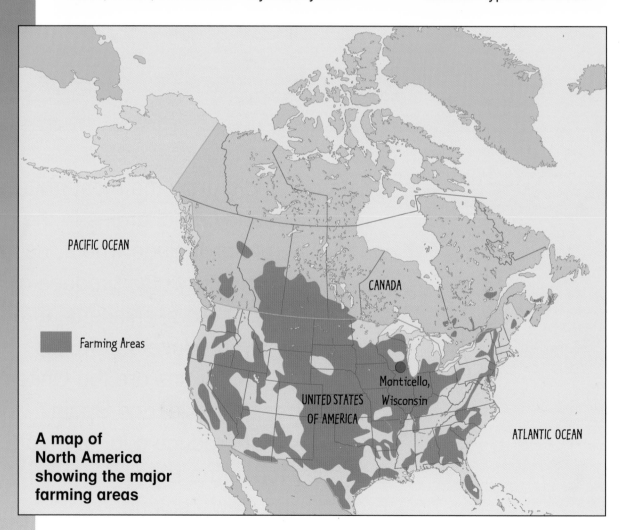

A map of North America showing the major farming areas

Farming Areas

PACIFIC OCEAN

CANADA

Monticello, Wisconsin

UNITED STATES OF AMERICA

ATLANTIC OCEAN

Glossary

alpacas Long-haired mammals originally from South America. They are raised mainly for their wool

citrus Fruits such as limes, lemons, grapefruits, and oranges

community A group of people who live, work, and play close together

construction Repairing or making homes, buildings, or roads

crop Plants grown on a farm to be sold or fed to farm animals

dairy foods Foods made out of milk such as ice cream, cheese, yogurt, sour cream, and butter

factories A business where machines are used to make something so it can then be sold. Also called a plant

farm products Something made or grown on a farm to be sold

fibers Long, thin thread-like parts of a plant

fuels Something that makes energy for heat, light, or to work a machine

harvest To gather crops that are fully grown and ready to use

irrigated Given water by using pipes, pumps, and hoses

Limburger cheeses Cheeses made originally in the Limburg region of Germany, Belgium, and the Netherlands

livestock Animals raised on a farm such as cows, pigs, and chickens

manure Animal waste

pests Insects that damage crops usually by eating them

plowed Soil that has been dug up by a plow

processing plants Factories that take a product and use it to make another product

raising Helping something to grow up by giving it food and a home

ranches Large farms that raise and sell animals such as cows or horses

rural areas Small, quiet places in the countryside

settlers First people to make homes in an area

sow To plant a seed

spun Pulled and twisted to make threads

Swiss cheeses Cheeses made originally in Switzerland

urban areas Built-up places such as a city or big town

Further Information

Further Reading

Berger, Melvin. *Scholastic True or False No 4: Farm Animals.* Scholastic Inc, 2008.

Dorling Kindersley. *Eyewitness Farm.* Dorling Kindersley Ltd, 2001.

Longenecker, Theresa. *Who Grows Up on a Farm?: A Book About Farm Animals and their Offspring.* Capstone Press, 2003.

Nelson, K. *Mighty Movers: Farm Tractors.* Lerner Publishing Group, 2002.

Wolfman, Judy. *Life on a Crop Farm.* Lerner Publishing Group, 2001.

Web Sites

Kids Farm
www.kidsfarm.com

Agriculture in the Classroom
www.agclassroom.org/kids

All About Farm Animals
www.kiddyhouse.com/Farm/

Farm Bureau Kids
www.farmbureaukids.com/

MooMilk: An Adventure into the Dairy Industry
www.moomilk.com/

Camp Silos (history of prairies and farming)
www.campsilos.org/

National Agricultural Services
www.ars.usda.gov/is/kids/index.html
www.agr.gc.ca/index.html

Index